Fighting!! Guidance 1
DANCE CLUB
STORY Keuk-Jin Jeon
ART Hye-Jin Eom
D0112025

CONTENTS

A Word From The Translator

Note 1

While most books don't need any additional background explanation, there is a rather large cultural gap between the US and Korean school life, hence this translator's note has been provided. It's highly suggested you read this prior to reading this book.

First of all, most minor notes will be denoted as a stand alone note on each page on which it occurs (rather than be listed in this section).

While not every school is plagued with an uncontrollable student delinquency, Korean middle schools and high schools are notorious for having student gangs roaming around each school. In a sense, it's a form of order brought to an otherwise chaotic clash of students everywhere and anywhere. At the beginning of each school year, most of these student delinquents will gather and challenge each other to fights to determine who is the 'Jhang,' a word meaning captain (but since the English word 'captain' didn't quite carry an edge to it, we translated the word to be 'boss'). And for the remainder of the school year, all the other delinquents basically follow around the Jhang and do whatever he says. This in a sense maintains some sort of order and hence, most teachers and school staff won't interfere or attempt to prevent these fights (provided they happen off-campus).

Now, to make things a bit more complex, there is actually a hierarchy to Jhangs. There is one Jhang per grade level and to be officially made a Jhang of any particular grade level, the Jhang of the grade above you must 'acknowledge' you (and this can be through various means).

In addition to managing the other delinquents in each grade, 'Jhangs' are also required to manage their 'territory.' A territory being a specified neighboring area around each school which is deemed to 'belong' to a particular school. This basically determines 'safe zones' from which students from a particular school can hang out without getting harassed by student gangs from other schools. This leads us into the next topic which is in regards to taking over territory belonging to other schools. Once Jhangs have been determined, some of the more arrogant Jhangs go around to other schools challenging other Jhangs. Beating other Jhangs basically brings more territory under their control. One thing to note is that under the rules of student gang engagements, virtually anything is allowed. While more credit is given to those who don't use weapons, bats, steal pipes, etc. aren't uncommon. In addition, there's really no such thing as a fair fight, hence, 1 on 1 fights are rare. In fact, most of these fights are more like mobs of people fighting (or a group of guys ganging up on one guy).

A Word From The Translator Continued...

What's interesting to note is that there are also female student gangs. All the same rules apply to them, but their reasons for fighting are a bit more delicate. Essentially, they fight solely to gain possession of territory. The thing is, what territory you control determines what territory you're allowed to pick up guys, hang out, etc...

Well that's the gist of it for the background information, but please don't take this the wrong way... While this does definitely exist, this delinquency is actually only comprised of a small percentage of the total student body. And no, the average person won't run into one of these gangs and get mugged on the streets... -_-;;

Well, if you haven't already been freaked out yet... please enjoy the book, it's really good (I swear it~!!).

Note 2

In this book there's something we translated as the 'Guidance Club.' While that is an accurate direct translation, the Guidance Club is something more like 'Student Council' in English. However, that in itself isn't a good translation as various things are very different and there is a separate system of student government body in Korea (in addition to the Guidance Club). Essentially, members of this club are supposed to be role models for other students and they fill miscellaneous rolls at everv school including hall-monitor positions, waiting by the school gate to take down the names of tardy students, etc.

In addition, a student isn't elected into his position as an officer of the Guidance Club. He has to earn his right to get in by exhibiting good grades and other merits. In other words, it's kind of similar to getting onto the Honor Roll... except much more difficult (as there are a limited number of seats). Also, most schools will only accept 2nd or 3rd year students into their Guidance Club. On a side note, the word for Guidance Club can also be translated as Guidance Department (which also makes sense).

쏴아아-
SSSSHH
STEP
철벅
허
HAAA
허
HAAA
허
HAAA

SEEING HOW THEY SENT YOU... IT SEEMS GUY-IN NEVER INTENDED ON LETTING ME WALK AWAY TO BEGIN WITH. I UNDERSTAND NOW.

Note : Sunbe is the Korean word for upperclassman in Korean. This word is commonly used to show respect amongst students, co-workers, and anyone within the same field or profession.

Fighting!! Guidance
FIGHT #1 : THE SUSPICIOUS LOOKING TRANSFER STUDENT

WHAT'RE YOU LOOKING AT FOOL?! YOU WANT SOME OF THIS, HUH?!
DOOOM
COME ON GUYS, GIVE ME A BREAK~ I'M NEW AROUND HERE!
HMP, WHAT A SISSY~ TURNING TAIL ALREADY...
TCH
THUD
THAT'S ENOUGH!
GASP~!!

DON'T YOU THINK 4 ON 1 IS A BIT UNFAIR?
WHO THE HELL ARE YOU?
I'M JUST A RANDOM PASSERBY.
YOU LITTLE SMARTASS, YOU WANT A BEAT DOWN AS WELL?!
CRACK
CRACK
I SUGGEST YOU GUYS GET LOST...
MY UNCLE WORKS PRETTY CLOSE TO HERE.

THE HELL YOU TALKING ABOUT?
WHAT ABOUT YOUR UNCLE, PUNK?
MY UNCLE'S A POLICE OFFICER,
AND HE'S STATIONED NEARBY.
IF YOU DON'T BELIEVE ME, I CAN CALL HIM OUT FOR YOU.
ONE PHONE CALL AND HE'LL BE HERE IN LESS THAN 3 MINUTES.

WHY YOU LITTLE...
TREMBLE
TREMBLE

WHY DON'T YOU END THIS NICE AND QUIETLY WHILE YOU STILL CAN?
KKK!
YOU'D BETTER WATCH YOUR BACK FROM NOW ON KID!
SWING
LET'S GO!

PHEW~ I THOUGHT THINGS WERE GONNA TURN REAL UGLY.
CONSIDER YOURSELVES LUCKY YOU BASTARDS! I WOULD'VE KILLED YOU!
EAT THIS!
fidget 버둥
fidget 버둥
YEAH, OK~ THANKS FOR YOUR HELP.
OH IT'S NOTHING ...
I GUESS I'M A LUCKY GUY OR SOMETHING~ I DIDN'T THINK I'D GET HELP, LET ALONE RUN INTO A CUTE GIRL ON MY FIRST DAY IN THIS NEIGH-BORHOOD.
FREEZE 움찔
YOU SHOULDN'T HANG AROUND IN THIS AREA.
THERE'S A LOT OF THEIR KIND AROUND HERE.
I CAN SEE WHY HE CAUGHT THEIR EYE...

HA HA~ OK THEN, I'M GONNA TAKE OFF SO...
HEY WAIT! HOLD UP..!
I WAS JUST CURIOUS...
CAN YOU TELL ME WHERE POONG RIM HIGH SCHOOL IS?
!!
HUH?
DID YOU SAY POONG RIM HIGH?
I THOUGHT I'D CHECK IT OUT TONIGHT SINCE I'LL BE STARTING THERE TOMORROW AS A NEW TRANSFER STUDENT...
?!!
NO... NO WAY!! YOU'RE TELLING ME YOU MADE IT INTO OUR SCHOOL?!
ROAR
SHRIEK~!!
HUH? THEN YOU'RE A STUDENT AT POONG RIM HIGH AS WELL?
What was that just now?!
I DON'T BELIEVE THIS...

OUR SCHOOL'S THE HARDEST TO GET INTO IN THIS AREA... HOW DID AN AIRHEAD LIKE HIM GET IN..?
I ALMOST MISTOOK YOU FOR GUY AT FIRST~
BY THE WAY, WHY ARE YOU WEARING CLOTHES LIKE THAT?
TREMBLE
I'M A 1ST YEAR STUDENT, WHAT ABOUT YOU? IF YOU'RE NOT DOING ANYTHING LATER, HOW ABOUT WE GET SOME...
I GUESS THIS SCHOOL MIGHT BE WORTH LOOKING FORWARD TO.
WELL, SEEING HOW CUTE GIRLS LIKE YOU GO THERE,
...
HA HA HA
UM... I'M NOT A...
부들 부들
TREMBLE
TREMBLE
HEY~!! WHAT THE HELL ARE YOU DOING FLIRTING WITH ME?!!
OH COME ON BABE~
I'M HYUN-HA GHANG AND I'M A 1ST YEAR STUDENT IN CLASS #4!!
WHAT? NO WAY!
MORE IMPORTANTLY, I'M A GUY DAMMIT!!
I'M TELLING YOU I'M A FREAKING GUY!!
WAVE

PAT
PAT
PAT
HUH~? YOU'RE RIGHT, YOU ARE A GUY!
SMACK
FUME
FUME
MAN, THIS IS HARD TO BELIEVE. WHAT KIND OF GUY LOOKS THIS CUTE..?
...?!
우당탕
TUMBLE
CLANG
쿵탕
CRASH
와당

STUDENT AFFAIRS OFFICE
HM? WHAT'S WITH THAT BUMP ON YOUR HEAD?
POONG RIM HIGH
I'M SURPRISED THEY LET YOU INTO THIS SCHOOL WITH THIS KIND OF SCORE ON THE ENTRANCE EXAM.
HE HE HE...
GETTING BACK TO THE SUBJECT...
OH THIS? IT WAS JUST SOME TRASH CAN THAT CAME FLYING OUT OF NOWHERE AND HIT ME ON THE HEAD...
SCRATCH
SCRATCH
A TRASH CAN?

HMM... LET'S SEE NOW~ WHICH CLASS SHOULD I STICK YOU IN? ACCORDING TO THIS, THE ONLY CLASS THAT ISN'T FULL IS...
...!
UM, ACTUALLY... I HAD A REQUEST...
HM? WHAT IS IT?
DOOOOM
HEY GUYS, IT LOOKS LIKE YOU'RE STUCK WITH ME FROM TODAY ON. I'M GHI-HAN SHIN...
CHATTER
CHATTER
LET'S GET ALONG, ALRIGHT KIDDOS~
웅성
I DON'T BELIEVE THIS...

Take a seat back there.
Oh, ok...
HMP~ THIS GUY LOOKS LIKE FUN...
HOW DID SOMEONE LIKE HIM GET INTO OUR SCHOOL?
WHAT A JOKE, HE LOOKS LIKE THE TYPE THAT CAN'T STUDY EVEN IF HIS LIFE DEPENDED ON IT.
I THINK YOU'RE RIGHT FOR ONCE...
YO~ WE MEET AGAIN!
DREAD
딩동
DING DONG
DENG DONG
뎅동

SEEING HOW OFTEN WE RUN INTO EACH OTHER...
MAYBE FATE IS PLAYING A HAND HERE, DON'T YOU THINK?
IF IT IS, THEN IT'S ONE UNLUCKY FATE.
DO ME A FAVOR AND GO AWAY...
HEY HEY... WHY THE COLD SHOULDER? I EVEN WENT THROUGH THE TROUBLE...
OF GETTING INTO THE SAME CLASS AS YOU.
I'D APPRECIATE IT IF YOU STOPPED ACTING LIKE I WAS YOUR FRIEND.
HEY~ ISN'T THAT GOING A LITTLE TOO FAR..?
...!
...!

YO, LET'S GO TALK OUTSIDE FOR A MINUTE.
WHO? ME?
DON'T GO WITH HIM!!
SLAM
IF YOU'RE THINKING ABOUT CAUSING TROUBLE, I ADVISE YOU TO STOP!

DON'T YOU THINK YOU'RE OVER REACTING A BIT MR. ALMIGHTY GUIDANCE CLUB OFFICER?
I WAS ONLY PLANNING ON SHOWING THE NEW GUY AROUND.
SHRUG
YOU NEED TO CHILL OUT SOMETIMES MAN~
IF HE DOESN'T WANT TO, THAT'S FINE WITH ME...
TURN
STROLL
STROLL
WHO WERE THEY?

THEY'RE THE TYPE THAT 'GOES OUTSIDE TO TALK' A LITTLE TOO OFTEN...
HE WAS PROBABLY TRYING TO SCOUT YOU AS ONE OF HIS LACKEYS.
HM... I WONDER WHY THEY'D TRY TO SCOUT SUCH AN INNOCENT LOOKING KID LIKE ME?
ANYWAYS, IF YOU DON'T HAVE ANY BUSINESS WITH ME, LEAVE ME ALONE.
...!
HEY, DON'T TELL ME YOU'RE STILL MAD ABOUT YESTERDAY ARE YOU?
......
GIVE ME A BREAK, ONLY SOUR OLD CHICKS HOLD GRUDGES LIKE THAT MAN~
DON'T TOUCH ME~!!
GRRR
PAT
NOW THAT I THINK ABOUT IT...
크~
KKK~!

HOW ABOUT YOU LET ME SEE IT ONCE JUST SO I CAN MAKE SURE?
I WON'T BELIEVE IT UNTIL I SEE IT WITH MY OWN EYES.
YOUR THING FELT A BIT TOO LARGE.
JUST ONCE MAN...
TREMBLE
TREMBLE
SHUT
OK, FOR ALL THE INTERIM GUIDANCE CLUB OFFICERS...
YOU BASTARD! STOP SAYING THAT KIND OF CRAP WITH SUCH A SERIOUS FACE!
OW~!!
SMACK
AND GET LOST WILL YOU!!

Note : Adding the word 'Sunbe' to a name shows respect towards that person. Please refer to the note on page 9.

OH, IT'S NOTHING IMPORTANT...
IT'S JUST THAT THERE'S SOME PSYCHO IN MY CLASS AND...
IS IT BECAUSE OF YOUNG-WOO BY ANY CHANCE?
HUH, WHAT DO YOU MEAN?
HEY YOU THERE~ TRANSFER STUDENT!

LET'S TALK FOR A MINUTE.

HA HA... I GET THE FEELING YOU WON'T TAKE NO FOR AN ANSWER...

I HEARD HE HANGS OUT WITH A LOT OF NOTORIOUS DELINQUENTS.
YOU SHOULD STAY AWAY FROM HIM.
IT'LL BE BEST IF YOU DON'T GET MIXED UP IN ANYTHING THAT INVOLVES HIM.

FOR SO-YHUN SUNBE TO BE GIVING ME A WARNING AND ALL, I GUESS HE'S NOT JUST SOME NEIGHBORHOOD BULLY.
SPLAT
HM?
WHA... WHAT WAS THAT?!
CLANG
KKK~!!

퍽 퍽
THUD
STOMP
퍽
STOMP
퍽
STOMP
퍼억
STOMP
퍽
WHAT THE HELL'S WRONG WITH YOU?! WHY WON'T YOU FIGHT?!
씩씩
FUME
TWITCH
TWITCH
RUSTLE
WHAT A WASTE OF TIME, HE'S JUST A BIG SISSY~!
RUB
SQUEEZE
주물주물
!!

IT TOOK A LOT TO GET TRANSFERRED HERE SO THAT I COULD GET A CLEAN START...
HEY BUDDY, DON'T YOU THINK THIS IS GOING A BIT TOO FAR ON THE NEW GUY?
WIPE
SHUT THE HELL UP~! YOU'RE NOTHING BUT TALK!!
THUD
KKK!!
WHAT DO YOU THINK YOU'RE DOING?!
!
!
!
HAAA
HAAA

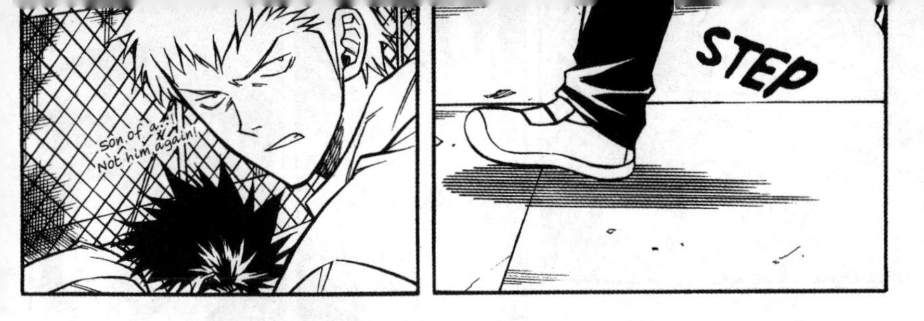
Son of a...!! Not him again!
STEP

저벅
STEP
STEP
저벅

ARE YOU OK?
HEY, DON'T WORRY ABOUT ME. IT'S NOT AS BAD AS IT LOOKS.

TURN
I THOUGHT I TOLD YOU TO STOP PICKING ON PEOPLE YOUNG-WOO!
...!
DO YOU REALLY WANT TO GET DRAGGED INTO THE DEAN'S OFFICE THAT BADLY?!
WHO DO YOU THINK YOU'RE TALKING TO BITCH?!
CRACK
SQUEEZE
JUST CAUSE I LET YOU HAVE IT YOUR WAY FOR A WHILE...
DASH
YOU THINK I'M SOME SORT OF PUSH OVER, PUNK?!

WOOSH
SWING

CRACK
CLENCH
SMACK

KKK~!!
CRASH
Y... YOUNG-
WOO..!!
STEP

IF YOU CAUSE ANY MORE TROUBLE,
THIS WON'T BE THE END OF IT NEXT TIME!!
YOU'RE NOT THE ONLY ONE WHO KNOWS HOW TO USE HIS FISTS.
DON'T!!
WHY YOU LITTLE..!!

LET THEM GO.
...!!
BUT WHY YOUNG-WOO..?
I SAID LET THEM GO!!

CAN YOU WALK?
......
HUH? OH, UM...
YEAH, OF COURSE ...
......
ARE YOU REALLY GOING TO JUST LET HIM GO? IF YOU DO THEN...
HMP! DON'T WORRY ABOUT IT, I HAVE SOMETHING IN MIND.

ARE YOU SURE YOU'RE OK? YOU DON'T WANT TO GO TO THE HOSPITAL OR THE NURSE'S OFFICE?
수근
CHATTER
CHATTER
수근
I'M FINE, I'M FINE~!
THIS IS NOTHING...
WHEN YOU COMPARE IT TO SOME OF THE OTHER THINGS I'VE BEEN THROUGH...
GEEZE... YOU REALLY ARE NOTHING BUT TALK...
HEY GIVE ME SOME CREDIT NOW~ I DON'T FIGHT ONLY BECAUSE I DON'T WANT TO.
IF I REALLY WANTED TO, I COULD TAKE OUT TRASH LIKE THEM WITH JUST ONE PUNCH.
IF YOU CAN'T EVEN FIGHT,
WHY DO YOU KEEP GETTING MIXED UP WITH GUYS LIKE THAT?
...!

THIS KIND OF STUFF ONLY HAPPENS...
BECAUSE YOU KEEP SAYING THINGS LIKE THAT~!
Hey foo~ You want some of this?!
I ONLY STEPPED IN BECAUSE I'M AN OFFICER OF THE GUIDANCE CLUB. IF I HADN'T STOPPED THEM...
...!
THAT'S RIGHT! YOU'RE IN THE GUIDANCE CLUB AREN'T YOU?
...
HM... THAT'S STRANGE, WHAT'S UP WITH THIS SCHOOL? AREN'T YOU ONLY A 1ST YEAR STUDENT?
MOST OTHER SCHOOLS ONLY ALLOW 2ND AND 3RD YEAR STUDENTS TO JOIN THE GUIDANCE CLUB, NO?
DON'T COMPARE OUR SCHOOL'S GUIDANCE CLUB TO OTHER SCHOOLS.
THE DEDICATION OUR SCHOOL'S OFFICERS PUT IN IS ON A COMPLETELY DIFFERENT LEVEL...
WHAT DO YOU MEAN?
DURING THE 2ND SEMESTER, 1ST YEAR STUDENTS CAN JOIN THE GUIDANCE CLUB AS INTERIM OFFICERS.

THEN AT THE BEGINNING OF THEIR 2ND YEAR, JUST A HANDFUL OF THESE INTERIM OFFICERS ARE PICKED TO BECOME FULL FLEDGED OFFICERS.
GOOD GOD... WHY MAKE SUCH A SIMPLE THING SO COMPLEX?
THAT'S WHY OUR SCHOOL'S GUIDANCE CLUB IS SO WELL KNOWN.
AND THAT'S NOT ALL. EVERYONE IN OUR CLUB IS SKILLED IN ONE FORM OF MARTIAL ARTS OR ANOTHER MAKING THEM IDEAL TO HANDLE ROUGH SITUATIONS.
ON TOP OF THAT, OUR CLUB EVEN RUNS INTER SCHOOL DISTRICT CONFERENCES.
IF YOU REALLY CONSIDER YOURSELF A MAN, DON'T YOU THINK THIS IS WORTH TRYING OUT FOR?!
TADAA
...

AH..! NOW I GET IT!
TAP
THE REASON YOU'RE DOING THINGS LIKE THIS...
IS CAUSE YOU HAVE SOME SORT OF MASCULINITY COMPLEX ISN'T IT?
FREEZE
뜨끔
YEAH, BUT WHY ELSE WOULD SOMEONE GO THROUGH ALL THAT TROUBLE?
I... I DON'T HAVE A FREAKING COMPLEX, DAMN YOU!!
SHRIEK
WELL THA... THAT'S BECAUSE...
MUMBLE
S... SOMEONE HAS TO... TO UPHOLD JUSTICE IN SOCIETY AND... AND...
MUMBLE
U HE HE HE~! YOU KNOW, WHEN YOU STAMMER LIKE THAT, YOU LOOK PRETTY CUTE TOO~
CREEP
DOOOM
PSSSSSH
WHY DID I EVEN BOTHER HELPING YOU?!
I hate myself for having helped him twice!
YOU'RE NOT SUPPOSED TO HIT INJURED PEOPLE DUMMY...

I CAN'T BELIEVE HIM... DOES HE ACTUALLY ENJOY MAKING FUN OF PEOPLE?
WEIGHT TRAINING
FOR GUYS WHO WANT TO BUILD A MASCULINE BODY
A MASCULINITY COMPLEX..? HMP! HE DOESN'T KNOW WHAT HE'S TALKING ABOUT!
RUSTLE
THERE!
SIGH...
DES
PAR
SLUMP

SIGH~ I'M BEAT, TODAY WAS SO BUSY.
DRAG DRAG
YEAH, THANKS. I'LL CATCH UP TO YOU OVER THERE.
HEY IS BONG-JOON THERE..?
YUP... HE JUST LEFT.

WOW, I DIDN'T KNOW IT WAS THIS LATE ALREADY.
IT'LL BE PRETTY TIGHT TRYING TO MAKE IT TO THE GYM BEFORE THEY CLOSE~
CREEP
CREEP
.....!!

NOW LOOK WHO WE HAVE HERE~!
HEY PUNKASS KID, I DIDN'T THINK I'D BE RUNNING INTO YOU HERE!

I TAKE IT YOUR UNCLE'S STATION IS QUITE A WAYS FROM HERE HUH?

WHAT DO YOU WANT?

STEP

HUH?! WHAT'RE YOU DOING HERE YOUNG-WOO?!
HE HE~ SURPRISED?
SINCE YOU'RE A GUIDANCE CLUB OFFICER, THERE'S NO WAY I CAN TOUCH YOU ON CAMPUS WITHOUT GETTING IN TROUBLE WITH THE TEACHERS.
...!!

Note : Hyung is a respectful way of refering to someone older. It's a direct translation of 'older brother.'

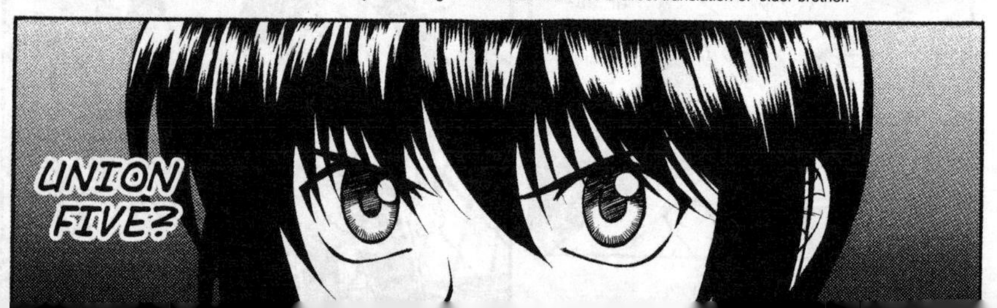

PAT 턱
I HEARD YOU WEREN'T TOO FRIENDLY TO MY BUDDY HERE.
WHY DON'T WE FIND OUT IF YOUR FISTS WORK ON ME HUH?
CRACK 우득
CRACK 우득
OH YOU DON'T HAVE TO WASTE YOUR ENERGY ON HIM HYUNG.
I'LL BE TAKING CARE OF HIM.
치잇
HMP
IT...
IT DOESN'T LOOK LIKE THIS WILL END QUIETLY...

IN THAT CASE...
SLIDE
DASH
I'LL ATTACK FIRST!!
KKK~!!
VOOSH
VOOSH
VOOSH
VOOSH
VOOSH

YOU LITTLE BASTARD~!!
WHOOSH
LURCH
탓
WHIFF
WHIFF
WHIFF
WHIFF
TAP
TAP
HE... HE'S NO JOKE! I THINK EVEN ONE OF HIS PUNCHES WILL KNOCK ME OUT.

ATTACK ME AGAIN LIKE EARLIER!!
YOU LITTLE PIPSQUEAK! IS DODGING ALL YOU KNOW HOW TO DO?!
DASH
SMACK
KKK~!!
THROB
THROB

SLIDE
THUD
CLASP
NOW I GOT YOU.
!!
HEY... THIS ISN'T FAIR!!
TAKE HIM!!
COME HERE BITCH!

SMACK
HOW WEAK, THIS IS SAD!!
SMACK
SMACK
SMACK
SMACK
KU HA HA HA~!!
SMACK
SMACK
KKK~!!
I'LL END YOU WITH THIS!!

AAH~ I REALLY DIDN'T WANT TO GET MIXED UP IN ANY FIGHTS HERE...
STOP
BUT I DON'T THINK I CAN JUST STAND BY AND WATCH MY NEW FRIEND GETTING ALL MESSED UP.
WHA... WHAT'S HE DOING?
HUH? WHAT'S THAT WUSSY DOING HERE?
I HAD A FEELING SO I FOLLOWED BEHIND JUST IN CASE...
SLIDE

TRASH LIKE YOU ALWAYS DO THIS KIND OF CRAP...
STEP
STEP
IF YOU DON'T GET LOST PUNK, YOU'RE NEXT!
THIS ISN'T A PLACE FOR SISSIES
LIKE...
...?!

SMACK
COUGH
CLANG

DAMN IT...
THUD
I REALLY JUST WANTED TO GO TO SCHOOL QUIETLY...
STEP
CREEP
YOU WANNA DIE?
HEY YOU..!
DIE? WHO ME?

GET HIM~!!
TURN
!
!

SMACK
SMACK

SMACK
SMACK
SMACK
SMACK
CRASH
THUD

!!
I... I DON'T BELIEVE THIS..!
SO WHAT'LL IT BE?
YOU WANT YOUR FACE ON THE PAVEMENT TOO?
저벅 저벅
STEP STEP
HMP! YOU'LL BE SORRY IF YOU THINK I'LL BE THE SAME AS THEM!
I'M GOING TO BE MADE A MEMBER OF UNION FIVE SOON!
HOW STUPID... YOU THINK JOINING SOME SCUM GATHERING LIKE THAT IS WORTH BRAGGING ABOUT?
SAY WHAT..?!

YOU BASTARD..!!
HOW DARE YOU TALK TRASH ABOUT UNION FIVE?!!
GRAB
I'LL TEACH YOU A THING OR TWO!!
TUG
RIP
SWING

A TATTOO?!
A DI... DIVINE MARK?!
D... DON'T TELL ME... HE'S ONE OF UNION FIVE'S...
HIGH CLASS?!
WHOOSH

COUGH
SKID
SMACK
CRASH
THUD
WHAT A HASSLE...
AND I JUST GOT THIS SCHOOL UNIFORM MADE TOO.
STARE~
...

WHAT? DON'T TELL ME THEY BEAT YOU SO BAD YOU CAN'T EVEN STAND.
...!
STARTLE
HUH? OH, UM..!
ALRIGHT, LET'S GO THEN.
TURN
W... WAIT!
JUMP
WHAT WAS ALL THAT JUST NOW?
THAT SKILL YOU USED ON THEM..!
WHAT, I THOUGHT I TOLD YOU ALREADY. I CAN TAKE OUT TRASH LIKE THEM WITH JUST ONE PUNCH.

WHY? IF I TOLD YOU, ARE YOU GOING TO GO LEARN?
TELL ME! HOW DID YOU GET POWER LIKE THAT?
DID YOU DO BOXING? OR SOME OTHER MARTIAL ARTS?
NO, YOUR POWER WAS INCREDIBLE JUST NOW. WITH POWER LIKE THAT YOU COULD..!!
HM...
WANTS TO GET STRONGER!!
WELL DUH! ANY GUY WHO CONSIDERS HIMSELF A MAN,
....
FINE, COME HERE.
Alright~
WHISPER
WHISPER
YEAH SO IF YOU WANT TO GET AS STRONG AS ME...
THUMP
THUMP

!!
YANK
GO ASK SOMEONE WHO CARES!!
MAN, WITH FIREPOWER LIKE THIS I DON'T SEE WHY YOU WOULD HAVE A MASCULINITY COMPLEX...
HM?
WHOA~ THIS MONSTER'S HUGE! IT REALLY DOESN'T SUIT A GUY LIKE YOU!
• • • • • • •
WHAT'S A LITTLE SOMETHING LIKE THAT BETWEEN GUYS..?
HEY HEY~ CALM DOWN~!
I'M GONNA KILL YOU~!! STOP RIGHT THERE!!

FIGHT #2 :
I'M JONG-SHIK MIN, THE BOSS OF THE 2ND YEAR CLASSMEN!

UWAA~ I THINK I'M GONNA BE LATE!!
DASH
HAAA
HAAA
DANG, WAKING UP EARLY'S ONE THING I'LL NEVER BE ABLE TO DO!
Note : In Korea, the school gates are closed and locked after the initial class bell.
I'LL BET THE SCHOOL GATES ARE ALREADY CLOSED BY NOW WHICH MEANS...
DASH
LET'S SEE NOW, THIS SIDE LOOKS AS GOOD AS ANY~
GRAB
THERE!

EH?
HM?
YO~ HELL OF A THING TO BE DOING, CLIMBING WALLS AND ALL FIRST THING IN THE MORNING~!
SMILE
SHUT UP! WHAT THE HELL DO YOU THINK YOU'RE DOING ANYWAYS?! COME TO SCHOOL EARLIER STUPID!
THEN WHAT ABOUT YOU KID?
...!
WHAT? KID?!

TAP
APPARENTLY, YOU DON'T RECOGNIZE WHO I AM...
POSE
I WANNA SEE YOU HERE FOR A BIT.
?
까딱 POINT
까딱 POINT
I'M JONG-SHIK MIN...
AND I'M THE BOSS OF THE 2ND YEAR CLASSMEN!!
ROAR
SO GET THAT STRAIGHT PUNK BEFORE YOU SAY ANYTHING TO ME NEXT..!!
SHOOT~ I THINK I'M GONNA BE REALLY LATE~
...
탁 탁 탁 DASH
HEY! YOU BASTARD! I'M TELLING YOU COME HERE!!
WHAT'S THIS~? I CAME BECAUSE SOMEONE SAID 'COME HERE' BUT TO THINK YOU'RE THE ONE WHO CALLED...
CREEP

I THINK IT'S BEEN OVER 25 YEARS SINCE SOME PUNK KID
CLIMBED OVER THE WALL AND ACTED SO BRAZENLY...
TAP
탁
TAP
OH CRAP~ IT'S THE STUDENT AFFAIRS DEAN..!!
PHEW~! I BARELY MADE IT BEFORE THE BELL...
SWING
WHOA~! THAT WAS CLOSE!
WHOOSH

I'M GOING TO BREAK YOU, YOU BASTARD!
WHAT ARE YOU DOING?
ARE YOU TRYING TO CATCH A BUG OR SOMETHING?
BUT WHY?
WHAT? OH YEAH~ THAT?
FUME
DON'T TELL ME YOU ALREADY FORGOT WHAT YOU DID TO ME YESTERDAY?!

YOU THINK I'M TRYING TO THANK YOU RIGHT NOW?!
OH STOP IT, YOU'RE EMBARRASSING ME...
WHAT ARE FRIENDS FOR IF THEY DON'T HELP EACH OTHER OUT WHEN THEY'RE IN DANGER..?
TREMBLE
TREMBLE
WHO SAID YOU COULD JUST STRIP MY PANTS OFF LIKE THAT YESTERDAY, HUH?!
KWAAAA
GEEZE... YOU'RE MAD JUST CAUSE OF SOMETHING LIKE THAT?
...A GIRL...
STOP
ALRIGHT ALRIGHT, GEEZE... NEXT TIME I'LL ASK BEFORE TAKING YOUR PANTS OFF.
MUMBLE
DON'T TAKE MY PANTS OFF, EVER~!!
ANYWAYS, I'M NOT LETTING YOU OFF THIS EASILY! LET'S GO OUTSIDE, NOW!
OH COME ON, IT WAS JUST A JOKE! DON'T BE SUCH A GIRL MAN... CHILL OUT OK?
DRAG

WHAT THE HELL DID YOU JUST SAY?
You really want to die today huh..?
TURN
WHAT, YOU'VE NEVER BEEN TO THE MEN'S BATH BEFORE? AFTER ALL, YOU HAVE TO TAKE YOUR CLOTHES OFF BEFORE GOING IN AND THERE ARE OTHER GUYS AROUND...
...!
HMM~ YOU DO HAVE A POINT...
CREEP
YEAH THAT'S RIGHT! IF YOU CAN'T TAKE THAT AS A JOKE, YOU'RE NOT EVEN A MAN!
URK!
NOW NOW, IF YOU REALLY THINK I WENT TOO FAR, I'LL APOLOGIZE, HAPPY?
PAT PAT
ALRIGHT, FINE...
SLIDE

!
!
HEY COWBOY~ JUST GETTING IN NOW?
STEP
...!

WHY DON'T YOU AND I GO TALK FOR A MINUTE?
STEP
LET'S SEE NOW, SO WHAT IS IT THAT YOU WANTED TO TALK TO ME ABOUT?
WHA... WHAT'S YOUR PROBLEM ..?!
YOU'D BETTER THINK TWICE IF YOU'RE THINKING ABOUT CAUSING TROUBLE ON CAMPUS!
SHUT THE HELL UP! IF YOU KEEP GETTING IN MY FACE I'LL WHOOP YOUR ASS REGARDLESS OF WHETHER OR NOT YOU'RE IN THE GUIDANCE CLUB!
GULP

BUT...
HEY! WHERE DO YOU THINK YOU'RE GOING?! CLASS IS ABOUT TO START!
HUH? MISS HYUN-HA?
DON'T WORRY ABOUT IT MISS HYUN-HA, I'LL BE BACK SOON.
TURN
YOU BASTARD!! I'LL KILL YOU!!
RUMBLE
KYA HA HA HA~!!
SHAKE
SHAKE
HEY~ PUNKS..!!

CLICK
WANT ONE?
SO WHAT IS IT YOU WANTED TO TALK ABOUT?
I GUESS I WAS STUPID NOT TO REALIZE IT SOONER...
YOU WERE HIDING YOUR SKILLS WEREN'T YOU?
I THOUGHT I ALREADY TOLD YOU, I'VE USED MY FISTS BEFORE...
ANYWAYS, IT WAS MY FAULT FOR NOT REALIZING IT EARLIER.
WHAT? THEN YOU CALLED ME OUT HERE TO APOLOGIZE?
WHY DON'T YOU JOIN MY CLIQUE?

I'M THE 1ST YEAR BOSS AT THIS SCHOOL. IF YOU JOIN MY CLIQUE, A LOT OF THINGS WILL BE MUCH EASIER FOR YOU.
HEY LOOK, IT'S TOO BAD BUT YOU'RE TALKING TO THE WRONG GUY.
...!
I TRANSFERRED TO THIS SCHOOL BECAUSE I WANTED TO GET AWAY FROM ALL THAT.
TURN
I HAD A FEELING IT WAS GOING TO BE ABOUT THIS
SOMETIMES I HATE BEING RIGHT.
SCRATCH
IF THAT'S ALL, I'M GONNA HEAD BACK TO CLASS.
WHY DON'T YOU THINK IT OVER SOME MORE BEFORE SAYING NO!
THERE'S PLENTY OF ADVANTAGES AND YOU HAVE NOTHING TO LOSE!
WHAT?
I'VE HAD ENOUGH ALREADY. I'M SICK AND TIRED OF KIDS HAVING LITTLE WARS...

AND I SUGGEST YOU STOP DOING THINGS TO ANNOY ME ALRIGHT?
THAT IS, IF YOU WANT TO KEEP BEING THE HOT SHOT BOSS AROUND HERE... GOT IT?
ANYWAYS, I JUST WANT TO GO TO SCHOOL QUIETLY SO DON'T TELL THE ROWDY BUNCH AT THIS SCHOOL ABOUT ME OK?
KKK
WHAT DID YOU SAY?!
YOU LITTLE SHIT! I'M GONNA..!!
......!!

COME ON MAN, TRY TO SMILE MORE AND LET'S JUST GET ALONG ALRIGHT?
PAT
YOUR BUSINESS WITH ME IS OVER RIGHT?
...
I'M GONNA HEAD DOWN FIRST THEN.
DO YOU REALLY THINK YOU'LL SURVIVE IN THIS SCHOOL IF YOU BECOME MY ENEMY?
I HAVE PLENTY OF SUNBES THAT SUPPORT ME.
SHAKE SHAKE
WHY YOU LITTLE...!
IF IT'S A CUTE LOOKING FEMALE SUNBE, BRING THEM MY WAY ANYTIME~!

TAP
TAP

I WONDER WHAT HE AND YOUNG-WOO TALKED ABOUT?

힐끔
PEEK

SCRIBBLE

IF YOUNG-WOO'S UP TO SOMETHING AGAIN...
...?

HEY MISS HYUN-HA~ IS SOMETHING TROUBLING YOU?
WHISPER
GOD DAMMIT! I WAS GONNA LET IT SLIDE THAT LAST TIME BUT...
JUMP
!
Ssshh~ Quietly!
흠칫!
GULP
IF YOU HAVE SOMETHING TO SAY TO YOUR FRIEND, CAN YOU DO IT ELSEWHERE PLEASE?
CHATTER
웅성
CHATTER

SWEET JESUS, WHAT THE HECK WERE YOU THINKING WHEN YOU STARTED YELLING LIKE THAT IN THE MIDDLE OF CLASS?
YOU'RE THE LAST PERSON I WANT TO HEAR THAT FROM SINCE IT'S YOUR FAULT TO BEGIN WITH...
IN ANY CASE, WHAT DID HE SAY?
HUH?
WHAT DID YOUNG-WOO TALK TO YOU ABOUT?
OH THAT? IT WAS NOTHING IMPORTANT... HE WANTED TO BE FRIENDS AND ALL.
THE TYPES HE ASSOCIATES WITH AREN'T TOO NICE. IF YOU DON'T BE CAREFUL, YOU MIGHT EVEN GET SERIOUSLY HURT.
IT'LL BE FOR YOUR OWN GOOD NOT TO HANG AROUND WITH HIM.

SMIRK
WHAT'S THIS? ARE YOU ACTUALLY WORRIED ABOUT ME?
!
DID YOU FORGET I'M IN THE GUIDANCE CLUB? AT THE VERY LEAST I DON'T WANT TO SEE SOMETHING BAD HAPPEN TO A FRIEND.
ANYWAYS, YOU DON'T HAVE TO WORRY. I DON'T HAVE THE TIME TO WASTE FOOLING AROUND WITH THEIR KIND... I'M BUSY ENOUGH AS IT IS TRYING TO GET BACK WHAT I'VE LOST.
WHAT'S SO FUNNY?
PAT PAT
WHAT?!
Are you making fun of me again..?!
I'M ONLY SMILING CAUSE YOU'RE SO CUTE. DO YOU HAVE A PROBLEM WITH THAT?

HUH? GET BACK WHAT YOU LOST?
OH MY, IS THAT YOU HYUN-HA?
IT IS YOU.
GASP
!
WHAT ARE YOU DOING OUT HERE IN THE MIDDLE OF CLASS?
I, UM... THAT'S...
MUMBLE MUMBLE
!
HE HE

OH MY~
OH ME, YEAH~! IT'S NICE TO MEET YOU.
CLASP
STARTLE
IS HE A FRIEND OF YOURS?
!
WHO ARE YOU CALLING A BUDDY?
And get your arm off me~!
I'M GHI-HAN SHIN AND I'M THIS RASCAL'S BEST BUDDY.
LURCH
DID YOU SAY YOUR NAME WAS GHI-HAN..?
IT'S JUST THAT I RECALLED HEARING THAT NAME BEFORE...
OH... IT'S NOTHING.
IS SOMETHING WRONG?

REALLY~? IT'S NOT EXACTLY A COMMON NAME... WHERE HAVE YOU HEARD IT BEFORE?
DING DONG
OH DON'T WORRY ABOUT IT, YOU GUYS WOULDN'T KNOW ABOUT HIM ANYWAYS...
DENG
DONG
AH~ DID THE BELL ALREADY RING?
...!
WELL, I HAVE TO RUN SOME ERRANDS FOR A TEACHER SO...
OH OK, BYE...
TAKE CARE~
STEP STEP
Hmm~

SO THAT'S THE TYPE OF GIRL YOU LIKE HUH?
STARTLE
-!!
WHE... WHEN DID I EVER SAY I... I LIKED HER..?!
THERE'S NOTHING TO BE EMBARRASSED ABOUT. YOU'RE PERFECTLY QUALIFIED!
SHAKE SHAKE
WHY DO I GET A BAD FEELING ABOUT THIS..?
I'M TELLING YOU THIS AS SOMEONE WHO'S ACTUALLY SEEN IT FIRST HAND!
WITH A MONSTER LIKE YOURS,
TRUST ME, YOU CAN SATISFY ANY GIRL!
ALRIGHT, THAT'S IT~!! STOP RIGHT THERE SO I CAN KILL YOU~!!
시끌
CHATTER
CHATTER
시끌
HUH? WHY ARE YOU BEING LIKE THIS? I WAS ONLY COMPLIMENTING YOU... HEY, COME ON~!
SQUABBLE
CHATTER
CHATTER
SQUABBLE
EXCUSE ME, YOU TWO..!!

GUIDANCE CLUB
UNION FIVE?
YEAH, YOU HAVEN'T HEARD SE-JOON?
...!
THE WORD IS THAT THEY'VE STARTED TAKING OVER ALL THE TERRITORIES AROUND THIS AREA AND THEY'RE PRACTICALLY AT OUR DOOR STEPS.
ARE THEY AFTER OUR SCHOOL AS WELL?
THAT I'M NOT SURE ABOUT,
BUT IF THAT'S THE CASE...

LET'S STOP.
THERE'S NO REASON TO WASTE TIME ON SOMETHING WE'RE NOT EVEN SURE IS REALLY HAPPENING.
AND IF IT'S CONCERNING UNION FIVE...
SLIDE
OH HEY SE-JOON AND SANG-WOO, WHAT ARE YOU GUYS DOING HERE~?
YO~ HOW'S IT GOING SO-YHUN?

DID SOMETHING INTERESTING COME UP?
YUP, TAKE A LOOK AT THIS.
Here...
TAP
JONG-SHIK'S NAME WAS ON THE TARDY LIST TODAY.
OH REALLY? HOW UNUSUAL... HE'S NORMALLY GOOD ABOUT NOT GETTING CAUGHT SNEAKING IN LATE.
HM~ I GUESS HIS IMAGE AS THE 2ND YEAR BOSS WILL SUFFER A BIT AFTER PEOPLE HEAR ABOUT HIM GETTING CHEWED OUT BY A TEACHER.
YEAH AND ON TOP OF THAT, HE GOT CAUGHT BY NONE OTHER THAN THE STUDENT AFFAIRS DEAN.
HA HA...

IT'D BE NICE IF THIS WAS JUST A LAUGHING MATTER...
I JUST HOPE HE WON'T GO AND CAUSE TROUBLE TO RELEASE SOME STEAM...
SLIDE
I THINK YOU WORRY A BIT TOO MUCH SOMETIMES.
I MET SOMEONE NAMED GHI-HAN SHIN.
OH BY THE WAY, I FOUND SOMETHING INTERESTING TODAY AS WELL.
!
!
WHAT?

WHAT?! YOU MEAN UNION FIVE'S GHI-HAN?!!
JUMP
WHERE DID YOU SEE HIM?!
NO NO,
NOT THAT GHI-HAN...
I THINK IT WAS JUST A COINCIDENCE BUT ONE OF OUR NEW 1ST YEAR STUDENTS HAS THE SAME EXACT NAME.
O... ONE OF OUR 1ST YEAR STUDENTS?
AFTER ALL, IT'S JUST NOT POSSIBLE FOR GHI-HAN FROM UNION FIVE TO BE JUST BE A 1ST YEAR STUDENT RIGHT?
YOU HAVE A POINT... IT ONLY MAKES SENSE THAT HE'D BE OLDER THAN US. SO AT THE VERY LEAST HE'D HAVE TO BE A 3RD YEAR STUDENT IF HE HASN'T ALREADY GRADUATED.

ANYWAYS, WHY DID YOU GUYS GET SO JUMPY WHEN I MENTIONED THAT NAME?
WHAT, DON'T TELL ME THIS IS THE FIRST TIME YOU'VE SEEN A SOCCER BALL~
I'M NOT ASKING THAT, I'M ASKING WHERE YOU GOT IT!
I BORROWED IT FROM THE SOCCER CLUB.
IF YOU'RE DONE EATING LUNCH, HOW ABOUT A GAME?
I'D RATHER READ A BOOK THAN WASTE TIME WITH YOU.
OH COME ON~ HERE, I'LL EVEN TELL YOU A LITTLE SECRET~
TAP
WHISPER
THEY SAY NOTHING BEATS SOCCER WHEN IT COMES TO GROWING CALF AND THIGH MUSCLES~
!
WHISPER

CHATTER
SMACK
CHATTER
WHAT?
YOU'RE ASKING ME TO TEACH A 1ST YEAR PUNK A LESSON?

JONG-SHIK HYUNG, Y... YOU SEE...
THE THING IS...
빠
SMACK
악
쿠당탕
KKK~!!
SPIT
CRASH
OUCH..!
HEY YOUNG-WOO!
DO YOU KNOW WHAT THE HELL YOU'RE SAYING RIGHT NOW?
YOU'RE THE 1ST YEAR BOSS.

AND YOU CALLED OUT YOUR SUNBE FROM HIS LUNCH BREAK.
WHY? BECAUSE YOU CAN'T EVEN HANDLE THE KIDS IN YOUR OWN GRADE?!
I... I'M SORRY.
I SUGGEST YOU GET YOUR ACT TOGETHER! OTHERWISE I'LL HAVE TO RECONSIDER...
WHETHER YOU'RE FIT TO BE THE 1ST YEAR BOSS OR NOT...
DAMN! I DON'T THINK JONG-SHIK HYUNG IS GOING TO HELP. IT'S TOO BAD SINCE I KNOW JONG-SHIK HYUNG CAN EASILY TAKE...
STEP
저벅
STEP
저벅

SMACK
DROP
YO~ SORRY ABOUT THAT~!
STRUT
STRUT
SINCE IT'S ALSO KIND OF YOUR FAULT FOR JUST STANDING THERE IN THE MIDDLE OF THE FIELD, WHY DON'T WE ALL CALL IT EVEN OK?
WHO'S THE BASTARD THAT KICKED THAT BALL..?!!
DOOOM
....

ALRIGHT THEN, SEE YA~!
HEY~ I GOT THE BALL!
HEY YOU, STOP!!
THAT'S THAT PUNK FROM THIS MORNING..!
GHI-HAN, YOU'RE REALLY ASKING FOR IT!!
!
YOU KNOW HIM?
IS THAT RIGHT?
YEAH! HE'S THE ONE I WAS TELLING YOU ABOUT EARLIER HYUNG...

RUB
I TAKE BACK WHAT I SAID EARLIER. I THINK I'LL TEACH THAT BRAT SOME MANNERS MYSELF!

WANTE
FIGHT #3
GHI-HAN
GETS CAUGHT

ALRIGHT~! I THOUGHT CLASSES WOULD NEVER END TODAY!!
HMP~ GOOD FOR YOU.
WELL OF COURSE, I WON A BET FROM THE SOCCER GAME,
KE HE HE HE
FOOOM?
SO I'M GETTING A FREE BURGER MEAL, COMPLIMENTS OF SOMEONE!
IT'S NOT FAIR AT ALL! IF YOU WERE THAT GOOD AT SOCCER, I SHOULD HAVE BEEN TOLD FROM THE START!
SLAM
NOW NOW... A REAL MAN DOESN'T GO BACK ON A PROMISE, RIGHT?

HMP~ I WOULDN'T HAVE AGREED TO THE BET IF YOU HADN'T BEEN SO PERSISTENT...
투덜
MUMBLE
투덜
MUMBLE
RUSTLE
STEP
HEY, COME OUT WITH ME FOR A SEC.
WHAT? YOU STILL HAVE MORE TO SAY?
I'M NOT THE ONE WHO HAS BUSINESS WITH YOU THIS TIME. IT'S JONG-SHIK SUNBE THAT WANTS TO SEE YOU.
JO... JONG-SHIK SUNBE?!

FOR A GIRL'S NAME, THAT DOESN'T SOUND VERY PLEASANT...
IS SHE PRETTY?
!
WHAT?
HUH? THEN THIS SUNBE ISN'T A GIRL?
WHAT THE HECK ARE YOU THINKING?! THERE'S NO WAY IN HELL JONG-SHIK WOULD BE A GIRL'S NAME!
IF THAT'S THE CASE, GO AND TELL HIM I'M SORRY BUT I DON'T SWING THAT WAY.
PAT PAT
YOU REALLY WANT TO DIE HUH?
IN ANY CASE, YOU'D BETTER LISTEN CAREFULLY!
JONG-SHIK SUNBE IS THE 2ND YEAR BOSS AT OUR SCHOOL AND...
HEY, HYUN-HA~ WHAT'RE YOU DOING? LET'S GO ALREADY, I'M FREAKING HUNGRY!
......

SON OF A..! THAT BASTARD NEVER LISTENS TO ME SERIOUSLY!
H... Hey Young-Woo...
TREMBLE
TREMBLE
TOO BAD BUT I DON'T ACCEPT REQUESTS LIKE THAT... LET THAT SUNBE OF YOURS KNOW OK?
ALRIGHT THEN, I'LL SEE YOU TOMORROW BUDDY!
GO LET JONG-SHIK HYUNG KNOW THE PUNK'S TRYING TO RUN...
WHY CAN'T WE JUST TAKE HIM ON OURSELVES? I DON'T SEE WHY WE NEED TO GET JONG-SHIK HYUNG'S HELP...
Yeah...

JUST DO AS I SAY DAMN IT!!
FREEZE
옴찔
STOP
THAT PUNKASS...
WHAT?!
FROM NOW ON, STAY AWAY FROM HIM.
BUT WHY? THAT BASTARD...
IT'S NOTHING YOU HAVE TO KNOW ABOUT!
ANYWAYS, DON'T GO MESSING WITH HIM UNTIL I CHECK UP ON SOMETHING FIRST...

HMP!..
I DON'T KNOW WHAT'S GOING ON,
BUT SINCE I PROMISED BONG-JOON HYUNG I WOULDN'T LAY A HAND ON HIM, I CAN'T FIGHT HIM MYSELF...
HEY, HAVE YOU ACTUALLY MET JONG-SHIK HYUNG YET..?
NO, WHO'S THAT?
THAT'S STRANGE... THEN WHY WOULD JONG-SHIK HYUNG CALL YOU OUT?
HOW WOULD I KNOW?

ARE YOU SURE YOU DIDN'T GO AND BEAT UP SOME KID ON SOME CORNER SOMEWHERE?
의심
SUSPICION
GEEZE... WHAT THE HECK DO YOU TAKE ME FOR?
I'M NOT THE TYPE OF IDIOT WHO GOES AROUND PICKING FIGHTS!
BUT OF COURSE I COULDN'T HELP IT THAT LAST TIME...
...!!
NOW THAT I THINK ABOUT IT...
ISN'T IT BECAUSE OF ME ALL THIS TROUBLE WITH YOUNG-WOO STARTED?
TO HELP ME THAT TIME, HE..!
AH!

YOU SHOULD STAY AWAY FROM YOUNG-WOO.
I HEARD HE HANGS OUT WITH A LOT OF NOTORIOUS DELINQUENTS.
THEN JONG-SHIK HYUNG GETTING INVOLVED IS ALSO..?!
IN THE END IT MEANS I'M RESPONSIBLE FOR GETTING MIXED UP IN ALL THIS...
I... I GUESS I WAS WRONG TO THINK HE WENT AROUND CAUSING TROUBLE.
HM? WHY DO YOU LOOK SO TROUBLED?
NO... IT'S NOTHING. I JUST HAD SOMETHING ON MY MIND...
SMILE
I'M TELLING YOU, DON'T WORRY ABOUT IT! GANGBANGERS LIKE THEM ARE ALL JUST TALK!

DOOOOM
CHATTER 웅성
CHATTER 웅성
CHATTER 웅성
Why isn't he coming? This is starting to piss me off~
THOSE GUYS OVER THERE ARE DEFINITELY STUDENTS FROM OUR SCHOOL...
CHATTER
DOOOM
와글
CHATTER
HMM~
THEY'RE HERE AS WELL?
SMIRK
SERIOUSLY, DON'T WORRY! WE CAN JUST SLIP OUT THE SCHOOL GATE AT THE REAR~

AS AN OFFICER IN THE GUIDANCE CLUB, I CAN'T JUST LET THIS..!!
T... THEN YOU'RE JUST GOING TO KEEP AVOIDING THIS?!
SMIRK
NO PROBLEM! ALL WE HAVE TO DO IS GET OUT BY CLIMBING OVER THE WALL!
WELL IF THAT'S WHAT YOU WANT, I GUESS WE'LL JUST MARCH STRAIGHT OUT THE MAIN ENTRANCE...
TURN
O..! OK, OK! WE'LL CLIMB THE WALL..!
REFUSING TO COME OUT WHEN IT'S ME OF ALL PEOPLE TELLING HIM TO.
THE LITTLE SHIT HAS GUTS DOESN'T HE?

IT'S BECAUSE HE'S SO STUPID HE DOESN'T KNOW WHO YOU ARE HYUNG.
HMP, I'LL GIVE HIM A LESSON TODAY
HE'LL NEVER FOR...
THUD
HYUNG! ARE YOU ALRIGHT?!
KKK~!
WHICH BASTARD THREW THAT..?!

쿠웅
SLAM
HYUNG~!!

HEY, ARE YOU ALRIGHT..?
끼잉
STRUGGLE
SLIDE
HUH? WHY DO SOME OF YOUR FACES LOOK SO FAMILIAR..?

HEY... HOW LONG ARE YOU GONNA SIT THERE..?!
WHOOPS! MY BAD, MY BAD!
STEP
SORRY ABOUT THAT. I WAS KIND OF BUSY TRYING TO AVOID SOME PSYCHOPATH NAMED JONG-SHIK SO...
!
CLASP
OH~ IS THAT SO? LET ME INTRODUCE MYSELF...
I'M A 2ND YEAR STUDENT HERE AT POONG RIM HIGH AND MY NAME HAPPENS TO BE JONG-SHIK MIN.
SMIRK

REALLY?
I DON'T THINK I HEARD YOU SO CLEARLY THE FIRST TIME~
MIND REPEATING WHAT YOU SAID EARLIER?
JONG-SHIK SUNBE!
...
SQUEEZE
YOU KNOW... THE WAY YOU TALK IS SO CUTE I ALMOST WANNA KILL YOU!
TREMBLE
TREMBLE
FUNNY, IF YOU ASK ME... IT ALMOST SEEMS THIS SCHOOL CHOOSES ITS BOSSES BY HOW DIRTY THEIR TEMPER IS...
HA HA HA
CRACK

UM, SUNBE...
HE ONLY RECENTLY TRANSFERRED TO OUR SCHOOL SO...
HE PROBABLY MADE A MISTAKE OR TWO BECAUSE HE'S NOT AWARE OF A COUPLE OF THINGS...
I'M SURE HE'S SORRY AND...
WHAT THE HELL DO YOU WANT?! YOU WANNA DIE TOO?
JONG-SHIK HYUNG ...
WHAT~? EVEN A PIPSQUEAK LIKE HIM IS AN OFFICER?
EH?
ACTUALLY, HE'S IN THE GUIDANCE CLUB.
WHISPER
UM, JONG-SHIK SUNBE...
YEAH, WHATEVER... JUST GET LOST BEFORE I CHANGE MY MIND!

IF YOU BOTHER US ANY FURTHER, I WON'T CARE WHAT CLUB YOU'RE IN!
GLARE
GULP
...!
HE'S RIGHT.
!
YOU CAN JUST BUY ME A BURGER TOMORROW INSTEAD.
....
WHAT IS HE THINKING AT A TIME LIKE THIS?
FROM THE LOOKS OF IT, I THINK THIS PARTY MIGHT TAKE A WHILE SO WHY DON'T YOU JUST HEAD ON HOME.

HMP! I DON'T KNOW ABOUT EVERYTHING ELSE BUT I HAVE TO ADMIT I LIKE YOUR SELF-CONFIDENCE.
I'LL TEACH YOU TO RESPECT YOUR SUNBES PERSONALLY...
FOLLOW ME... AND DON'T THINK ABOUT RUNNING!
WOW, REALLY! I'M ACTUALLY LOOKING FORWARD TO THIS....
GHI-HAN...
WAVE
NO MATTER WHAT, I WON'T FIGHT SO DON'T WORRY ABOUT IT...
STEP
STEP

'NO MATTER WHAT I WON'T FIGHT'?
THEN...
-!!
I CAN'T JUST ABANDON HIM~!!
THUD
I HAVE TO FIND SOMEONE..!
DASH
SOMEONE THAT CAN HELP..!!

SLAM
쾅-
HAAA
HAAA
TE-JOON SUNBE...
WHAT'S WRONG? AND WHAT'S WITH THAT DISAPPOINTED LOOK ON YOUR FACE..?

UM, TE-JOON SUNBE... DO YOU KNOW WHERE THE CLUB PRESIDENT OR SANG-WOO HYUNG IS BY ANY CHANCE?
WHY'RE YOU LOOKING FOR THEM?
THE THING IS, UM... A FRIEND OF MINE GOT DRAGGED OUT BY JONG-SHIK SUNBE AND...
!!
YOU MEAN THE 2ND YEAR STUDENT JONG-SHIK MIN?!
YES... AND SO I CAME LOOKING FOR SOME HELP...

WHAT ARE YOU, AN IDIOT?!
SLAM
STARTLE
WHAT ARE YOU THINKING BRINGING PROBLEMS LIKE THAT HERE?
...!!
DON'T YOU KNOW WHO HE IS?! JONG-SHIK IS PRACTICALLY THE BOSS OF THIS ENTIRE SCHOOL!
IF WE GO AGAINST HIM, WE'LL BECOME HIS ENEMY!
BUT MY FRIEND GOT CALLED OUT EVEN THOUGH HE DIDN'T DO ANYTHING WRONG...
HOW DO YOU KNOW THAT? THE ONLY REASON SOMEONE WOULD GET DRAGGED OUT IS CAUSE HE DID SOMETHING STUPID IN THE FIRST PLACE.

TE... TE-JOON SUNBE!
GO HOME. THE GUIDANCE CLUB ISN'T HERE TO HELP YOU CLEAN UP AFTER YOUR FRIEND'S MISTAKES!
WHAT'S UP? DID SOMETHING HAPPEN?
SA... SANG-WOO SUNBE!!

VS
FIGHT #4 A STAND OUT WAY OF SIGNALING

STEP
저벅
STEP
저벅
HEY SUNBE, HAVEN'T WE GONE FAR ENOUGH?
SHUT THE HELL UP!
GLARE
WHOA~ HE'S SO TOUGH AND MEAN~!
SON OF A...!
BUT STILL...
THIS IS KIND OF A SURPRISE... I HEARD THAT THIS SCHOOL DIDN'T HAVE A GANG...

SCRATCH
HMM... THEN I WONDER WHY I HEARD RUMORS LIKE THAT?
WELL, I GUESS THAT'S NOT THE CASE HUH?
ARE YOU STUPID OR SOMETHING? WHAT KIND OF A SCHOOL DOESN'T HAVE A GANG?
STOP
TWITCH
WAIT, DON'T TELL ME,
NO ONE'S HEARD OF YOUR GANG CAUSE YOU'RE ALL SO WEAK, IS THAT IT?
LOOKING AT YOUR RESPONSE, I GUESS I'M RIGHT HUH?
YOU KNOW YOU'RE DIGGING YOUR OWN GRAVE RIGHT NOW HUH?

THAT'S NOT IT DUMBASS! IF ONLY THAT DAMN GUIDANCE CLUB WASN'T AROUND...
HEY YOU, YOUNG-WOO! SHUT YOUR TRAP!!
STARTLE
O... OK!
YOU REALLY WANT TO PUSH YOUR LUCK DON'T YOU?
STOP
IS IT CAUSE YOU REALLY WANT TO KNOW WHAT IT FEELS LIKE TO DIE?
JUST MY LUCK, INSTEAD OF A CUTE GIRL I'M STUCK WITH A GORILLA FACE THAT WON'T EVEN LET ME TALK...
WHINE
SHAKE
울컥

HEY PUNK..! YOU THINK I'M SOME KIND OF PUSHOVER?!
OH REALLY? THEN YOU'RE SAYING YOU'RE ONE TOUGH COOKIE EH?
POINT
WHY YOU LITTLE..!
YOU THINK I'M SOME NOBODY THAT ONLY ACTS BIG ON CAMPUS?!
I'M JONG-SHIK!!
WHO DO YOU THINK I AM?!
POONG RIM HIGH'S 2ND YEAR BOSS!!
POINT
WHAT?
WELL... WE'LL FIND OUT WON'T WE? EXCUSE ME FOR A SEC~!
TREMBLE TREMBLE
ANY BASTARD WHO MESSES WITH ME IS AS GOOD AS DEAD!

SMACK
WHERE'S THE BITCH THAT THREW THIS?!
GASP
STARTLE
LOOK, IT LANDED RIGHT ON HIS HEAD, SUNBE~
KWAAAA
끼야아

BLACK MERCEDES... BLACK SUITS... CREW CUTS... AND MUSCULAR BUILDS...
THESE GUYS ARE 100% MAFIA!!
!!
WHAT THE HELL IS THIS?! WHERE'S THE SHITHOLE THAT THREW THIS?!
FUME
FUME
WHA... WHAT ARE MAFIA GUYS DOING IN A PLACE LIKE THIS?!!
!!
WHY? WHAT'S WRONG WITH THROWING A BAG OR TWO EH?
STARTLE
OH, UM... THAT'S... THAT'S MY...

WHAT DID YOU SAY KID..?
SO, UM... THAT'S...
WHAT THE HELL YOU STARING AT HUH?
SHRIEK~!!
WAVE WAVE
YOU FAT ASSES!!
OK SUNBE! SHOW US YOUR SKILLS! SHOW US HOW TOUGH YOU ARE!
SHOVE
I'M SURE YOU CAN TRASH LITTLE PUNKS LIKE THEM WITH JUST ONE PUNCH RIGHT?
A-DUH~

SO WE LOOK THAT WEAK HUH?
I SEE HOW IT IS...
CRACK
CRACK
OH REALLY...
UM, NO..! THIS IS... UM, IT'S JUST A...
WHAT? JONG-SHIK?

YEAH, AND SO THAT'S WHAT HAPPENED.
ALRIGHT. I'LL CONTACT AS MANY OF OUR GUYS AS POSSIBLE.
ACTUALLY, IT'S A BIT MORE COMPLICATED THAN THAT.
TE-JOON FOUND OUT ABOUT THIS.
TE-JOON DID?
YOU KNOW HOW HE IS...
I HAD TO PULL RANK WITH HIM AND MADE HIM SIT QUIETLY FOR NOW...
OK, GOT IT... THEN I'LL DO THAT.
OK, HYUN-HA'S COMING BACK SO I'LL CALL YOU AGAIN LATER.

SO HE WASN'T THERE EITHER?
HMM...
YEAH, I THINK THEY ALREADY WENT SOMEWHERE ELSE.
FINE THEN, WE'LL TRY SPLITTING UP TO LOOK FOR THEM.
HERE, TAKE THIS.
TOSS
SE-JOON'S CELL'S IN THE ADDRESS BOOK,
SO IF YOU FIND ANYTHING GIVE HIM A CALL.
THANKS SUNBE, I'M SORRY ABOUT CAUSING ALL THIS TROUBLE...

WHAT ARE YOU SAYING? WE'RE OFFICERS IN THE GUIDANCE CLUB. OUR POLICY ISN'T TO TURN DOWN PEOPLE WHO COME LOOKING FOR HELP.
BUT IF THAT'S TRUE, THEN I DON'T THINK I'M QUALIFIED TO BE AN OFFICER.
—!
AFTER ALL, I LEFT A FRIEND IN DANGER AND RAN AWAY BY MYSELF.
THAT'S NOT TRUE...
YOU MADE A TOUGH CHOICE IN A DIFFICULT SITUATION, AND YOU MADE THE RIGHT CHOICE.
IN ANY CASE, LET'S HURRY AND LOOK FOR YOUR FRIEND.
WHO KNOWS WHAT'S HAPPENING TO HIM AS WE SPEAK?

HM?
IS SOMEONE TALKING ABOUT ME? I WONDER WHY I'M GETTING SO ITCHY ALL OF A SUDDEN?
SCRATCH
WHOOSH
THIS IS ONE SIMPLE WAY OF GETTING THEM OFF MY BACK BUT I ALMOST FEEL GUILTY.
OH WELL, IT'S NOT LIKE THOSE MAFIA GUYS WILL KILL THEM OR ANYTHING, RIGHT?

WHOA~!!
THUD
WHA... WHAT THE..?! WHERE'D HE DROP IN FROM?
CREEP
JUST LIKE I THOUGHT... THINGS IN LIFE AREN'T SO EASY AFTER ALL.
YOU LITTLE BITCH..!
DON'T THINK YOU MADE IT OUT OF THIS ONE JUST YET!!
RISE

I GET THE FEELING THEY'RE IN THIS AREA SOMEWHERE...
UWAAA~! HURRY, RUN!!
—!!
STOP YOU MAGGOTS!! WE'RE GONNA EAT YOU ALIVE!!
RUMBLE
HUH? ISN'T THAT..?

SMACK
CRASH
TAP
GET YOUR ASS BACK UP PUNK!!
MY MY... YOU'VE GOT ONE HELL OF A PUNCH THERE~

HOW ABOUT WE CALL IT EVEN NOW?
YOU'VE BLOWN OFF YOUR STEAM RIGHT?
HE HE...
TWITCH
SON OF A..!
YOU THINK THIS IS A GAME BITCH?!!
WHERE'S YOUR MOUTH NOW, HUH PUNK?!!
KKK!!
THUD

HAAA
?
VOOM
RISE
THERE'S A LIMIT TO EVERYTHING.
BUT..!
HEY LOOK...
SINCE YOU'RE MY SUNBE, I WAS GONNA LET YOU HAVE YOUR WAY WITH ME.

WHAT?
I SUGGEST YOU STOP THIS NOW... CAUSE IF YOU PUSH ME ANYMORE, I CAN'T GUARANTEE ANYTHING.
WHAT'D YOU SAY?
SO IF I PUSH YOU SOME MORE...
STEP
WHAT IS IT EXACTLY...
CREEP
THAT YOU'RE GOING TO DO, HUH?!!
SMACK

THE ONLY THING YOU KNOW HOW TO USE IS YOUR FREAKING MOUTH!
CLENCH
WAIT! JONG-SHIK SUNBE!!
STOP
멈칫!
HMP, IF THAT'S THE WAY YOU WANT IT...
TURN

HAAA
HAAA
HUH? WHAT'RE YOU DOING HERE..?
STOP
...!
STEP
STEP
...!
WHAT DO YOU THINK YOU'RE DOING RIGHT NOW? DIDN'T I TELL YOU TO GET LOST?

YOU THINK BEING A GUIDANCE CLUB OFFICER GIVES YOU THE RIGHT TO GET IN MY WAY?
PLEASE STOP THIS... YOU'VE ALREADY DONE ENOUGH HAVEN'T YOU?
YES ACTUALLY, I DO!
AT THE VERY LEAST, I CAN'T JUST LET SOMETHING LIKE THIS HAPPEN IN FRONT OF ME!
I'M AN OFFICER IN THE GUIDANCE CLUB.
YOU LITTLE BITCH..! YOU WANNA DIE TOO, IS THAT IT..?!

H... HEY... STOP FOOLING AROUND. THAT GUY HAS ONE MEAN FIST.
IF HE REALLY WANTED TO, HE COULD WIPE THE FLOOR WITH YOU!
I'M SORRY ABOUT EARLIER.
?
WHAT I DID WAS UNACCEPTABLE...
I'M A GUIDANCE CLUB OFFICER AT POONG RIM HIGH.... AND STILL I LEFT YOU ALONE IN DANGER AND RAN AWAY BY MYSELF.
HEY..! WHAT ARE YOU THINKING?! THIS ISN'T THE TIME FOR THIS!

HURRY, RUN!
I'LL HOLD HIM OFF FOR AS LONG AS I CAN!!
HEY..! WHAT ARE Y..!!
SMACK

FIGHT #5 THE PURPOSE OF THE GUIDANCE CLUB

YOU THINK I'M GONNA JUST LET YOU WALK OUT OF HERE?! HUH?!
THAT DAMNED CLUB AIN'T GONNA SAVE YOU IF YOU KEEP SAYING CRAP LIKE THAT!!
WIPE
JONG-SHIK SUNBE, NO MATTER HOW MAD YOU GET,
YOU CAN'T SOLVE YOUR ISSUES WITH VIOLENCE!
WHAT?!
!

PLEASE, LET'S STOP THIS NOW AND ALL OF US JUST WALK AWAY.
YOU LITTLE..!
WHO DO YOU THINK YOU'RE TALKING TO BITCH?!
THUD
HEY! WHAT DO YOU THINK YOU'RE..?!

DON'T... DON'T EVEN THINK ABOUT IT!!
CLASP
WHAT?!
ISN'T THAT YOUR GOAL? TO NOT FIGHT AND TO BE JUST A REGULAR STUDENT?
!!
I SAW YOU FIGHTING THAT LAST TIME SO I KNOW HOW GOOD YOU ARE.
AND UP TILL NOW, YOU HAVEN'T SHOWN AN INKLING OF WANTING TO FIGHT YOURSELF.

HYUN-HA... YOU..!
YOUR HOPES AND CONVICTIONS... I'LL PROTECT THEM FOR YOU!
DON'T WORRY ABOUT ME. I'M A GUIDANCE CLUB OFFICER.
THIS IS WHAT WE DO... IT'S SOMETHING THAT HAS TO BE DONE!

HMP..! IN THE END, IT JUST MEANS YOU'RE BEING A DUMBASS BECAUSE OF THAT SON OF A BITCHING CLUB!
FINE, WHATEVER! I'LL MAKE SURE TO MAKE YOU FEEL THE MISTAKE YOU'RE MAKING WITH YOUR BODY!!
CRACK
THUD
SMACK

KKK!!
WHOOSH!
SMACK
KKK..!!
SLIDE

SLAP
TAP
KKK!
STEP
IF YOU KEEP GETTING HIT LIKE THAT YOU'RE REALLY GOING TO LOSE SOME SCREWS UP IN THAT HEAD OF YOURS!!
THAT'S ENOUGH YOU RETARD!!

SHOVE
I'M NOT GOING DOWN THIS EASILY!
YOU'D BETTER NOT FIGHT!!
!
I'M A GUIDANCE CLUB OFFICER!
I'LL PROTECT YOUR CONVICTION...
비틀
WOBBLE
SAY WHAT YOU WANT SHITHEADS.
WHAT IS THIS GUY..?
WHY'S HE SO..?

IT DOESN'T CHANGE THE FACT I'M GONNA BEAT BOTH OF YOU SENSELESS!
!!
CLASP
CLENCH
NO! DON'T..!!

VOOSH
PHEW
!!
RUB
SO YOU'VE BEEN HIDING YOUR SKILLS HAVE YOU..?
INTERESTING...

IN THAT CASE, NO MORE HOLDING BACK!!
JOCK
SLAP
THAT'S AS FAR AS THIS GOES!
!
!
FREEZE
멈칫
SE... SE-JOON SUNBE!
HEY JONG-SHIK PUT A STOP TO THIS, NOW!

YOU'RE FINALLY... HERE...
LURCH
THUD
HYUN-HA! HEY~! GET A GRIP!!
STEP
저벅
ARE YOU PLANNING ON GETTING IN MY WAY SE-JOON?
저벅
STEP
DO YOU REALLY THINK I'M JUST GOING TO SIT THIS OUT
WHEN YOU PUT ONE OF OUR 1ST YEAR OFFICERS IN THAT CONDITION?

IT'S THEIR FAULT FOR PISSING ME OFF IN THE FIRST PLACE!!
WHY NOT PUT AN END TO THIS NOW THEN? YOU'VE HAD YOUR WAY WITH THEM RIGHT?
WHAT?!
THERE'S SUCH A THING AS TAKING IT TOO FAR. YOU'VE HAD YOUR WAY WITH THEM, WHY NOT STOP BEFORE IT GETS OUT OF HAND?
OR IS IT THAT YOU MISS BEING EXPELLED FROM SCHOOLS AND YOU WANT TO BE TRANSFERRED AGAIN?
ARE YOU THREATENING ME RIGHT NOW?!
I'M JONG-SHIK MIN DAMMIT!!
YOU THINK A THREAT LIKE THAT IS GONNA SCARE ME?
POINT

Note : Hoobae is the opposite of sunbe; a respectful word/marker to indicate someone who is ranked lower than you in some type of ranking system (ie professions, grade level, etc.).

BUT YOU..!
POINT
IF I EVER CATCH YOU WHILE YOU'RE ALONE, YOU'RE DEAD!
HMP..!
I'M SORRY ABOUT ALL THE TROUBLE...
ARE YOU ALRIGHT HYUN-HA?
NO, YOU DID VERY WELL TODAY. WHAT YOU DID WAS VERY BRAVE.
STEP

LEAN
YOU MORE THAN PROVED YOUR QUALITIES TODAY. WITHOUT A DOUBT, YOU'RE ONE OF POONG RIM HIGH'S FINEST GUIDANCE CLUB OFFICERS.
KEEP UP THE GOOD WORK, HYUN-HA!
PAT
I WILL!
OH THAT'S RIGHT! ARE YOU ALRIGHT?
!
THUD
KKK..! ALL... ALL OF A SUDDEN, MY STOMACH IS STARTING TO HURT!!

WHA... WHAT SHOULD WE DO?! DO YOU WANT TO GO TO THE HOSPITAL?
HOLD ON! I'LL BE RIGHT BACK WITH ONE!!
I... I THINK I'LL BE FINE IF I CAN GET A DRINK SOMEWHERE... PREFERABLY A SODA... ONE OF THOSE CHERRY COKES TO BE MORE EXACT...
WHAT AN INTERESTING SICKNESS. ONE THAT GETS HEALED BY DRINKING SODA, CHERRY COKE TO BE MORE EXACT WASN'T IT..?
TURN
HEY LOOK SUNBE, THERE'S JUST ONE THING I WANTED TO ASK.
!
YOU'D HAVE TO BE ONE GULLIBLE GUY TO BELIEVE SOMETHING LIKE THAT ACTUALLY EXISTS.

WHAT DO YOU MEAN BY THAT?
FOR WHAT PURPOSE DID YOU MAKE THESE POLICIES YOUR OFFICERS FOLLOW?
TRYING TO HELP ME... AND HE SAYS IT'S BECAUSE OF THIS GUIDANCE CLUB BULLSHIT.
THAT FOOL... HE PRACTICALLY GOT KILLED
...
WHY DO YOU ENFORCE THESE TYPES OF POLICIES?
WHY DO YOU ASK?

I'M ASKING BECAUSE I KNEW SOMEONE ONCE THAT WAS DOING THE SAME STUPID THINGS AS YOU.
DEPENDING ON YOUR ANSWER, I'LL KNOW WHETHER OR NOT THIS PLACE IS WHERE I BELONG.
YOU'RE ONE EGOTISTICAL FRESHMAN YOU KNOW THAT?
THE PURPOSE OF THE GUIDANCE CLUB IS TO HELP GUIDE STUDENTS
IN THEIR DIFFICULT PATHS IN LIFE.
I FIND THAT HARD TO BELIEVE. HYUN-HA JUST SAT THERE TODAY GETTING BEAT DOWN LIKE A RAG DOLL.
AND FOR WHAT? HE HAD NOTHING TO GAIN FOR IT... THAT JUST MAKES HIM A FOOL, NOTHING MORE.
HAVE YOU LIVED YOUR ENTIRE LIFE LIKE THIS? NOT TRUSTING ANYONE..?

LIKE I SAID, THE GUIDANCE CLUB HAS ONLY ONE PURPOSE.
HOW PEOPLE EXPRESS THEIR DEDICATION FOR ACHIEVING THAT GOAL IS UNIQUE FOR EVERYONE.
HEY~ I FOUND ONE FOR YOU!!
DASH
AND CONSIDERING ALL THAT, I HAVE HIGH HOPES FOR HIM.
UNFORTUNATELY, HE DOES HAVE ONE FLAW... HE DOESN'T HAVE THE POWER HE NEEDS TO CARRY OUT HIS OWN WILL YET.
!
IF THAT ANSWERS YOUR QUESTION, I'LL BE TAKING OFF NOW...
ARE YOU TAKING OFF SE-JOON SUNBE?
I'LL SEE YOU TOMORROW KID.

HERE, IT'S THE SODA YOU WANTED.
HUH?
OH RIGHT... THE SODA.
WHAT WERE YOU TALKING TO SE-JOON SUNBE ABOUT?
HE WAS JUST TELLING ME WHERE ALL THE GOOD BURGER JOINTS WERE.
OH THAT?
!

DON'T TELL ME YOU STILL WANT TO EAT WITH YOUR FACE ALL MESSED UP LIKE THAT.
WHAT'RE YOU SAYING? A GROWING MAN NEEDS TO EAT! ESPECIALLY AFTER USING UP SO MUCH ENERGY!
Note : Eating after having a fist-fight is probably the last thing the average person wants to do. The inside of one's mouth generally gets very 'ripped-up'. Attempting to eat after getting punched in the mouth generally means you'll be tasting more blood than food (and it'll also sting… especially if you drink soda).
ALRIGHT ALRIGHT, WE'LL GO, WE'LL GO..! GEEZE~
!
SMIRK
WHAT? DID JONG-SHIK SUNBE HIT YOU SO MUCH YOUR BRAIN GOT ALL SCREWED UP? WHY ARE YOU LAUGHING?
NO, I WAS JUST THINKING... HOW I MUST BE A PRETTY LUCKY GUY TO HAVE RUN INTO SOMEONE LIKE YOU...

SOMEONE LIKE ME?
WHY? WHAT KIND OF NEIGHBORHOOD DID YOU LIVE IN BEFORE?
BACK BEFORE I CAME HERE...
I REALLY DON'T WANT TO GO BACK TO THE WAY I USED TO LIVE...
IT WAS THE KIND OF PLACE...
THAT DIDN'T HAVE CUTE GIRLS LIKE YOU MISS HYUN-HA. YUP, NOT EVEN CLOSE~
STUPID GAY BASTARD! YOU MAKE ME SICK!!
W... WAIT..! DON'T LEAVE ME BEHIND~! WHAT ABOUT MY BURGER~?!

FIGHT #6
WHICH UNDERWEAR
SHOULD I CHOOSE?

WHAT? A HIGH CLASS?
THAT'S RIGHT GYONG-HOON HYUNG.
HAVE YOU HEARD ANY WORD IF ANYONE IN THE HIGH CLASS IS IN THIS NEIGHBORHOOD?
THE HELL YOU TALKING ABOUT? WHY WOULD SOMEONE IN THE HIGH CLASS BE IN A USELESS PLACE LIKE THIS?

HYUNG, THE TRUTH IS, I SAW SOMEONE WITH A DIVINE MARK RECENTLY.
PPHHHTTT
YOU GOTTA BE KIDDING ME. ARE YOU SURE YOU WEREN'T JUST MISTAKEN?
COUGH COUGH
NO I'M SERIOUS! I'M POSITIVE IT WAS A DIVINE MARK!
SO WHO WAS THIS GUY THAT HAD THIS MARK?
ACTUALLY... IT WAS SOME GUY WHO GOES TO POONG RIM HIGH.
SMACK

MAN, YOU HAD ME THERE FOR A SEC. I GUESS I WAS THE IDIOT FOR LISTENING SO SERIOUSLY!
TAP
OUCH!
WHY THE HELL WOULD SOMEONE IN THE HIGH CLASS BE GOING TO SCHOOL?
ESPECIALLY, TO A SISSY SCHOOL LIKE PHOONG RIM?!
YES... I WASN'T SURE MYSELF SO...
CREEP
IT'S PROBABLY JUST SOME KID WHO HEARD ABOUT UNION FIVE AND GOT AN IMITATION TATTOO.
CLICK
THA... THAT'S WHAT I THOUGHT TOO HYUNG.
ALRIGHT, ENOUGH OF THIS NONSENSE. SO WHAT ABOUT THAT ERRAND I GAVE YOU?
YEAH, I HAVE SOMEONE IN MIND AND HE'S EXACTLY THE TYPE YOU ASKED ME TO FIND.
THE ONLY REASON THE POONG RIM GANG ISN'T BETTER KNOWN IS BECAUSE THE GUIDANCE CLUB THERE IS SO STRONG AND...

HEY DUMBASS, SPARE ME THE STORY OK? I DIDN'T ASK YOU TO GIVE ME A DAMNED SPEECH!
YOU THINK I CAME OUT HERE TO HEAR YOUR EXCUSES?
NO HYUNG, OF COURSE NOT!
STOP BY WITH THAT KID AS SOON AS YOU CAN... THE ONE YOU HAVE IN MIND!
HUH?
LET'S SEE IF HE'S REALLY GONNA TO BE USEFUL OR NOT.

RUMBLE
HEY, CHECK IT OUT! IT'S A NEW RECORD!
THIS MUST BE THE FIRST TIME EVER I MADE IT TO CLASS THIS EARLY~!
SLIDE
HEY GUYS~ WHAT'S UP?
?
TURN
SHRINK

HUH?
!
SHRINK
TURN
HEY DID SOMETHING HAPPEN?
CREEP
MY... MY BAD... I HAVE SOMETHING I NEED TO TAKE CARE OF SO...
DASH
?
SMACK
!!
I WONDER WHAT'S GOING ON?
SCRATCH

KE KE KE
WHAT DO YOU WANT?
I HEARD JONG-SHIK SUNBE KICKED YOUR ASS GOOD YESTERDAY.
LURCH
STOP
BEING ALL SMILEY AND HAPPY HAPPY THE DAY AFTER YOU GET WHOOPED... AREN'T YOU THE TOUGH TROOPER?
YEAH, I THINK I GET IT NOW...
YOU TOLD EVERYONE TO MAKE ME FEEL LIKE A LONER, IS THAT IT?

HOW WOULD I KNOW?
KE KE
IF YOU ASK ME, I THINK IT'S JUST THAT PEOPLE DON'T LIKE YOU...
WHAT ARE YOU UP TO NOW?
!
!!
YOU'D BETTER NOT BE THINKING ABOUT CAUSING TROUBLE DURING CLASS!
WELL, WELL... IF IT ISN'T MR. JUSTICE.
LET'S GO...
KE KE KE
WHAT IS IT?
HEY, I WANT TO TALK TO YOU FOR A MINUTE.

HOW YOU FEELING? YOU GOT BEAT PRETTY BAD YESTERDAY YOU KNOW?
STEP
STEP
THAT'S NOT THE ISSUE HERE.
?
FROM THE LOOKS OF IT, I THINK EVERYONE ALREADY FOUND OUT YOU GOT CALLED OUT BY JONG-SHIK HYUNG YESTERDAY.
AND I WON'T BE TOO SURPRISED IF YOUNG-WOO AND HIS IDIOT FRIENDS WERE THE ONES SPREADING THE NEWS.
?
?
WHAT'S SO PROBLEMATIC ABOUT THAT?
ONCE PEOPLE HEAR THAT YOU'RE ON THE BLACK LIST OF MOST OF THE THUGS AT SCHOOL,
NO ONE'S GOING TO WANT TO BE YOUR FRIEND.
BECAUSE IF THEY HANG AROUND YOU, THEY'LL GET BLACK LISTED AS WELL.
HMM... YOU HAVE A POINT!

HEY THEN, IS IT REALLY OK FOR YOU TO BE HANGING AROUND ME AS WELL?
THE WORST PART ABOUT IT IS THAT I DON'T THINK THEY'RE GOING TO LET UP ABOUT IT IN JUST A FEW DAYS OR EVEN WEEKS.
AT THIS RATE, YOU'LL END UP BEING A COMPLETE LONER FOR YOUR ENTIRE HIGH SCHOOL LIFE.
I'M A GUIDANCE CLUB OFFICER! I'M NOT GOING TO JUST SIT AROUND AND LET YOU GET TREATED LIKE THIS!
I'M USED TO IGNORING THOSE TYPES ANYWAYS...
COME ON MAN, THERE'S NO REASON TO GET THAT WORRIED.
ONCE THEY HAVE THE WHOLE SCHOOL AGAINST YOU, YOU DON'T KNOW WHAT CAN HAPPEN!
THEN ARE YOU WILLING TO THROW AWAY YOUR HIGH SCHOOL SOCIAL LIFE AND JUST BE A LONER THE ENTIRE TIME?
SHRUG
MAN~ YOU REALLY ARE ONE WEIRD KID~!
CAN'T YOU EVER BE SERIOUS?!
IT'S YOUR SOCIAL LIFE THAT'S ON THE LINE HERE!!

OR WAIT, DON'T TELL ME YOU'RE PLANNING ON GOING BACK TO YOUR OLD SELF... FIGHTING AND THROWING YOUR FIST AROUND WITH THE REST OF THE THUGS?!
YOU KNOW, SOMETIMES YOU REALLY GO OVERBOARD WITH YOUR IMAGINATION.
AND IT'S NOT LIKE THIS IS THE END OF THE WORLD OR ANYTHING.
WHY DON'T YOU JOIN THE GUIDANCE CLUB?
EH..?
I THOUGHT ABOUT IT ALL DAY YESTERDAY...
AT THE RATE YOU'RE GOING, THEY'LL CLASH WITH YOU EVERY CHANCE THEY GET.
THE ONLY SURE WAY TO MAKE THEM STOP HARASSING YOU IS TO JOIN THE GUIDANCE CLUB.
I'M GONNA HAVE TO PASS ON THAT ONE. I'M NOT EXACTLY THE PUBLIC SERVICE TYPE OF GUY.

AND...
SPLASH
OH WHOOPS... MY BAD~
I HAD NO IDEA SOMEONE WAS DOWN THERE~!

TAKE YOUR TIME NOW~ CLASS DOESN'T START FOR ANOTHER FEW MINUTES YOU HEAR?
...
CLANG
ARE YOU OK..?
SMASH
HMP, THAT LITTLE PUNK KNOWS HOW TO BE REALLY CUTE SOMETIMES..!
YOU REALLY SHOULDN'T BREAK SCHOOL PROPERTY LIKE THAT.
ROAR
HELLO~?! THERE'S SOMETHING MORE IMPORTANT AT HAND HERE!!

DID YOU SEE THAT FOOL?
HA HA HA
THAT BIG SISSY... HE WON'T EVEN DO ANYTHING ABOUT IT.
BUT HEY YOUNG-WOO, WHY DID YOU GET OUR SUNBES TO HELP,
INSTEAD OF TAKING CARE OF HIM YOURSELF?
I SAY WE DRAG HIM OUT AND KICK HIS ASS SOME MORE.
HMP, THAT'S NOT A BAD IDEA...
HM?
RING
HELLO?
YEAH IT'S ME. I WANT YOU TO COME OUT FOR A BIT, THERE'S SOMEONE IMPORTANT THAT WANTS TO MEET YOU.
OH IS THAT YOU BONG-JOON HYUNG?

...AND SO...
HE DECIDED TO JOIN THE GUIDANCE CLUB.
IS THAT RIGHT..?
LET ME FORMALLY INTRODUCE YOU TO HER. THIS IS SO-YHUN SUNBE... SHE'S THE VICE-PRESIDENT OF THIS CLUB.
HUH? THEN YOU'RE SO-YHUN?
HM? DO YOU KNOW ME OR SOMETHING?
DO YOU BY ANY CHANCE KNOW JONG-SHIK SUNBE?
YEAH WHAT ABOUT IT?

THIS IS GREAT! I HOPE WE CAN BECOME GOOD FRIENDS!
CLASP
OH, UM... SURE.
WHAT ARE YOU DOING? DID YOU ALREADY FORGET WHY WE'RE HERE?
HE HE...
OF COURSE I DIDN'T FORGET, WE CAME TO MEET CUTE GIRLS~!
KONK
WE CAME TO GET YOU INTO THE CLUB STUPID!
OH THAT, YEAH~ I CAME TO GET INTO THE CLUB!
PUTTING EVERYTHING ELSE ASIDE FOR A MINUTE...
I'M ASSUMING YOU ALREADY KNOW THE BASIC REQUIREMENTS FOR ENTERING THE GUIDANCE CLUB RIGHT?
HUH? WHAT REQUIREMENTS?
YOU JUST HAVE TO SCORE GRADES WITHIN THE TOP 20 PERCENTILE OF YOUR GRADE LEVEL.
DON'T WORRY, IT'S NOTHING HARD.
WHAT?

NORMALLY FOR 1ST YEAR STUDENTS, YOUR GRADES DURING THE 1ST SEMESTER ARE USED FOR THE ENTRANCE QUALIFICATION,
BUT SINCE YOU RECENTLY TRANSFERRED IN, YOU CAN PROBABLY JUST USE YOUR MID-SEMESTER EXAMS AS...
THANK YOU FOR EVERYTHING UP TILL NOW AND...
꾸벅
BOW
W..! WAIT!!
UM... YOU DON'T HAVE TO GIVE UP ALREADY...
WHAT DO YOU THINK YOU'RE DOING?! LEAVING ALL OF A SUDDEN AND ALL..!
I DON'T WANT TO HEAR IT! YOU'RE THE ONE WHO DRAGGED ME THERE IN THE FIRST PLACE!
DO YOU ACTUALLY THINK GETTING WITHIN THE TOP 20 PERCENTILE IS JUST SOME WALK IN THE PARK FOR ME?!
I BARELY PASSED THE ENTRANCE EXAM FOR THIS SCHOOL!
BUT...
HEY JACKASS!!

YOU STILL REMEMBER BONG-JOON HYUNG RIGHT?
HE WANTS TO SEE YOU LATER TONIGHT. YOU KNOW THAT THERE'S NO USE RUNNING RIGHT?
ARE YOU STUPID OR SOMETHING? I DON'T HAVE TIME TO FOOL AROUND WITH SCUM LIKE HIM.
THAT'S RIGHT! GHI-HAN'S GOING TO BE BUSY STUDYING FOR EXAMS!
EXAMS?
HEY, WHEN DID I SAY I WAS GOING TO..?!
GHI-HAN'S PLANNING ON JOINING THE GUIDANCE CLUB.
!!

PU HA HA HA HA~!!
PU..!
AND WHAT IF I DO GET IN HUH?
YOU..? JOIN THE GUIDANCE CLUB..? WHAT A JOKE~!
HA HA HA
하하하
WHAT?
THIS HAS TO BE THE STUPIDEST THING I'VE EVER HEARD~!
I'M GUESSING YOU'VE DECIDED TO JOIN CAUSE WE'RE PICKING ON YOU A BIT,
BUT GIVE ME A BREAK~! YOU THINK JUST ANY DUMB PUNK LIKE YOU CAN GET INTO OUR SCHOOL'S GUIDANCE CLUB?

LOSER RUNS A LAP AROUND THE SCHOOL IN JUST HIS UNDERWEAR! HOW ABOUT IT?
A LAP AROUND THE SCHOOL IN JUST UNDERWEAR?
WHAT? ARE YOU THAT UNCONFIDENT?
THAT'S RIGHT. IF I DON'T GET IN, I RUN,
BUT IF I DO GET IN, YOU RUN.
YOU LITTLE BASTARD...
!
HMP, YOU'RE THE ONLY ONE WHO'LL BE REGRETTING THIS IN THE END!

IF YOU'RE SO SURE THEN SHAKE ON IT!
FINE BUT YOU'D BETTER NOT CHICKEN OUT LATER!
HEY YOUNG-WOO ARE YOU REALLY SURE ABOUT THIS? IF HE REALLY ENDS UP GETTING IN THEN...
WHAT ARE YOU STUPID? STOP WORRYING... ANYWAYS, I OVERHEARD SOME OF THE TEACHERS SAYING THEY'RE MAKING THIS COMING TEST ESPECIALLY HARD TO SEPARATE OUT THE STUDENTS.
HMP! WE'LL SEE WHO'LL BE LAUGHING IN THE END! HE'S GONNA REGRET HAVING OPENED HIS YAP!

HEY, YOU WERE PRETTY COOL BACK THERE..!
W... WHA...
WHAT AM I GONNA DO NOW?! I'M GONNA END UP RUNNING A LAP IN JUST MY UNDERWEAR~!
PANIC
HUH?
DAMMIT, I WONDER WHICH UNDERWEAR WILL MAKE ME LOOK LESS LIKE A LOSER~?
MEN'S CATALOGUE
Lc CATALOGUE
...
DON'T TELL ME YOU MADE THAT BET WITHOUT EVEN THINKING...
WHAT THE HELL WAS THERE TO THINK ABOUT? I WAS JUST SO PISSED OFF, I WAS SAYING WHATEVER!
SIGH...
WELL, REGARDLESS... YOU WERE STILL PRETTY COOL BACK THERE.

TO BE CONTINUED IN
FIGHTING! GUIDANCE VOLUME 2!!

Art by Jeon Keuk-Jin
Story by Eom Hye-Jin

English Version Print
May 2005

Produced by

infinitystudios

www.infinitystudios.com

6331 Fairmount Avenue Suite #1
El Cerrito, CA 94530

Fighting! Guidance © Keuk-Jin Jeon / Hye-Jin Eom 2004
Fighting!! Guidance
infinitystudios
www.infinitystudios.com
Story by Keuk-Jin Jeon
Art by Hye-Jin Eom
Want More Fight?
VOLUME 2 AVAILABLE AUGUST 2005
Presented By Infinity Studios

Story by Eun-Jeong Kim
Art by Seung-Man Hwang
Zippy Ziggy
Fake it like THIS!!
Volume 1
Now Available
Presented by
infinitystudios
www.infinitystudios.com
Zippy Ziggy © Eun-Jung Kim / Seung-Man Hwang 2004

Na Na Na Na © Show=Tarou Harada 2003
comics ONE www.ComicsOne.com
infinitystudios
www.infinitystudios.com
Infinity Studios Presents
Show=TAROU HARADA's
NANANANA
WE CAN SENSE DANGER COMING A MILE AWAY...
WE LEGIONS ALWAYS LOOK OUR BEST...
WE'RE ALWAYS RELIABLE, DEPENDABLE, AND NEVER BREAK DOWN.
KYAA~!
ALLOW ME TO INTRODUCE THE LATEST IN ANDROID TECHNOLOGY KNOWN AS 'LEGIONS'.
WE MUST PROTECT THE CITIZENS OF THIS FAIR CITY!
OK, JUST LET ME FINISH THIS BOX OF DONUTS FIRST...
SMACK
Volume 1
Now Available

WAIT~
WIGGLE じた
WIGGLE ばた
It takes a great deal to survive in outer space...
HURRAH! SAILOR
Volume 1
Story by Rintaro Koike
Character Designs by Kouichi Kiga
Comic by Katsuwo Nakane
Now Available
TWITCH
TWITCH
AHA HA HA
PANIC PANIC
FUMBLE FUMBLE
But it takes even more to survive in outer space with this bunch.
comics ONE www.ComicsOne.com
infinitystudios
www.infinitystudios.com
Hurrah! Sailor © KATSUWO NAKANE 2004
Hurrah! Sailor © RINTARO KOIKE 2004
Hurrah! Sailor © DATAM POLYSTAR 2004

Infinity Studios Presents
Masakazu Iwasaki's
POPO CAN
Super Trouble Heroine?
Volume 1
Now Available
comics ONE www.ComicsOne.com
infinitystudios
www.infinitystudios.com
Popo Can © Masakazu Iwasaki 2003

Studios
Ahn No-Uhn
Death & Rebirth...
Good & Evil...
Café
infinitystudios
www.infinitystudios.com
Café Occult © Ahn No-Uhn / Oh Rhe Bar Ghun 2003
Volume 1
Now Available

NOW © Sung-Woo Park 2001
infinitystudios
www.infinitystudios.com
INFINITY STUDIOS PRESENTS
SUNG-WOO PARK'S
NOW
LIMITED EDITION
VOLUME 1 RE-RELEASE
AVAILABLE
SEPTEMBER 2005
PLEASE VISIT
WWW.INFINITYSTUDIOS.COM
FOR MORE INFORMATION

infinitystudios
www.infinitystudios.com
INFINITY STUDIOS PRESENTS
SUNG-WOO PARK'S
NOW
LIMITED EDITION
VOLUME 6
AVAILABLE
SEPTEMBER 2005
PLEASE VISIT
WWW.INFINITYSTUDIOS.COM
FOR MORE INFORMATION
NOW © Sung-Woo Park 2002

BamBi

Volume 1
Now Available

One day a stubborn young lady finds herself out in the middle of nowhere, and she can't remember a thing! Her name, where she's from, and why she was almost about to drown in a pond. But fate would have it though that a dashing young man with blonde hair and a wing for his right arm would rescue her.

Somehow, deep down inside, this young man puts her at ease, and as she had lost all of her memories, she asks him to name her. With a face expressing the mixed emotions of sadness, remorse, and hope, he names her Bambi...

Story & Art by
Park Young Ha

infinitystudios
www.infinitystudios.com

Bambi © Park Young Ha 2003

Art by : Park Sung Woo
Story by : Oh Rhe Bar Ghun

"Trapped and injured, that's when Cathy must have seen me... She called for me with all her might, but I just couldn't hear her...

She must have felt betrayed when I didn't return to rescue her. I guess there's no way she could forgive me..."

Available September 2005

Peigenz © Park Sung Woo

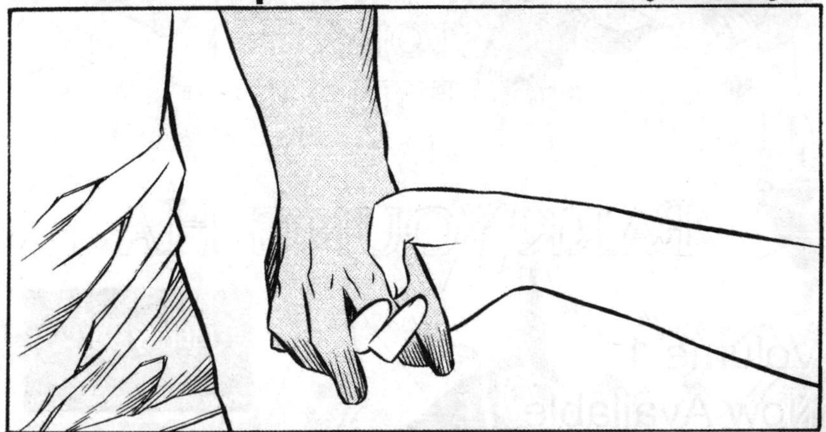

The Missing White Dragon
Infinity Studios Presents
Story Collections by
Park Young Ha
infinitystudios
www.infinitystudios.com
Volume 1
Now Available
The Missing White Dragon © Park Young Ha 2003

Infinity Studios Presents

Story & Art By Lee Ru

Volume 1 Now Available

Volume 1
Now Available

Infinity Studios Presents
Yu Sue Mi's

Animal Paradise

infinitystudios
www.infinitystudios.com
Animal Paradise © Yu Sue Mi 2003